Mischief

Mischief

A Collection of Juvenile High-Jinx

Written by Stephen W. Wasz
Illustrated by Greg Wimmer

iUniverse, Inc.
New York Lincoln Shanghai

Mischief
A Collection of Juvenile High-Jinx

Copyright © 2006 by Stephen Wasz

iUniverse books may be ordered through booksellers or by contacting:

iUniverse
2021 Pine Lake Road, Suite 100
Lincoln, NE 68512
www.iuniverse.com
1-800-Authors (1-800-288-4677)

The views expressed in this work are solely those of the author and do not necessarily reflect the views of the publisher, and the publisher hereby disclaims any responsibility for them.

ISBN-13: 978-0-595-40615-9 (pbk)
ISBN-13: 978-0-595-84982-6 (ebk)
ISBN-10: 0-595-40615-7 (pbk)
ISBN-10: 0-595-84982-2 (ebk)

Printed in the United States of America

This book is dedicated to Nance and Irene, a couple of great moms that were truly "diamonds in the rough."

Contents

Mud, Muck and The Pool Below 1

Tunnel Tales 5

BOW...19

Linksters on The Boulevard 37

MUCK, MUD, AND
THE POOL BELOW

My first clear recollection of existence is of the frolicsome, mischievous afternoon my older brother (Jimmy, age four) and I (age three) spent lobbing tiny dirt bombs onto the neighbor's freshly swept, pristine pool deck and watching them roll into the pool. Maybe my selective memory is indicative of some delinquent predisposition, or maybe flinging mud was just an extremely good time. I don't know.

We lived in the Piedmont area, atop a hill with a rather steep pitch, like most of the hills in Alameda County. It had rained that morning, and the dusty slope upon which our house sat had become a quagmire of gooey, brown California real estate. Picture a double-dip rocky road ice-cream cone with caramel syrup dripping down its sides; the landscape imitated that perfectly (though I'm sure the cone tasted much better). Rumor has it that backyards are supposed to have grass, but our backyard wouldn't be considered a poster-child for Better Homes, because the lawn's greenery was patchy at best. I think this was partly because we had dug a big hole back there and pulled plenty of grass out of the ground to line our "sandbox." Whatever the reason, the backyard was in perfect pigsty condition after it rained that morning. Jimmy and I pulled out our plastic trucks—his red and mine white—and we were ready to play.

When I say, "play," I don't mean calmly pushing hand-sized miniature trucks and making *vroom-vroom* noises. I'm talking truly interactive stuff. Jimmy and I climbed atop the plastic cabs of the oversized toy trucks and rode those bad boys about fifty yards, right down the sloppy slope, into a puddle of muck. Then we rolled around awhile, pretending to be crash-test dummies. Not only did we make a mess, we became one.

After only a couple of trips, Jimmy and I were soaked with grime and covered in mud. We got tired of lugging our goo-caked trucks back up the hill and decided to take a little rest. That's when the trouble began.

We were no different from most children; quietly sitting in one place for a prolonged period of time (over thirty seconds) was not in our repertoire of everyday behavior. Jimmy threw the first fistful of the thick, gloppy, caramel-colored slop. It was a direct hit; I could feel the grime in my nostrils. I returned fire, and the mud fight ensued. The battle raged for only a brief period before we decided to concentrate on inanimate objects instead of each other; mud balls hurt.

The Eastwood family had just moved. Their built-in swimming pool sat just below our house, at the base of our sloping backyard, and the new owners had just cleaned the pool area in preparation for a housewarming party. As a matter of fact, Jimmy and I sat on a bluff that directly overlooked the pool's neatly swept concrete deck. It was an irresistible temptation to lob down mud balls and watch them explode on the beige patio, then trickle into the clear blue pool water, only to disintegrate into tiny, dark clouds that quickly faded away as they sank to the bottom. We were delighted to discover that if we simply tossed the dirt clod out about five feet, it would drop directly on target! Consequently, we were content to just sit there, blissfully lobbing fistfuls of nitrogen-rich California soil into the new neighbor's pool. To us, this was more fun than a whole week of cartoons with no commercials. Unfortunately, our new neighbor didn't share in our blissful enjoyment.

When the lady of the house saw her formerly pristine pool deck speckled with little blotches of mud, she must've thought she was a victim of some malicious act of vandalism. But then, when one of our muck missiles exploded before her very eyes, she must have assumed she had caught the malicious caper in progress. The only problem was that from her window, our perturbed neighbor could only see that the onslaught was coming from the hill above, not who was throwing the mud. She probably opened the back door and yelled something, but we didn't pay any attention. (Imagine that: kids not paying attention.) We just kept on chucking that mud, peppering the pool with dirt and having a great time doing it.

This new lady of the house took the whole thing a little too seriously for my liking, especially since I was the one throwing the mud balls. She must've thought the pool was under attack from some deranged, dirt-clod slinging vandals, because she called the cops. Evidently, she didn't know that small children were chucking the dirt bombs, and that for them, derangement was just a developmental stage.

The law-enforcement officials were quick to defend the personal property of the taxpaying citizen and promptly dispatched two boys in blue to the scene of the crime. The officers arriving on the scene tracked our mud-ball trajectory from the neighbor's pool up the hill to our backyard, where they found Jimmy and me squatting in a mucky puddle of California earth, gleefully throwing fistfuls of mud all over the place. They didn't have to do any DNA testing to determine that the mud in the pool matched the mud on our faces. Instead of just making us quit and leaving it at that, these duly deputized officers of the law, now self-appointed social workers, had to make a big production out of it. They informed our new neighbor that they had apprehended the perpetrators. They then escorted us to the front door of our house and rang the doorbell, summoning my mother away from bathing my two-year-old brother, only to display Jimmy and I covered from head to toe in mud, in the company of two uniformed police officers and our agitated new neighbor.

The first officer politely explained to my mother that her children were guilty of violating Section 437 of the California Penal Code 634-7—throwing mud balls in the neighbor's pool—and this type of mischievous activity could someday blossom into something worse. Our new neighbor, the victim of this dastardly deed, told our mother to take better care of us, explaining with self-righteous indignation that children today needed to learn respect for personal property. She explained that this lesson needed to be taught early—especially to boys.

"First it starts with mud balls as toddlers," she went on, "then spitting on sidewalks at ten; then loud, annoying music when they're teenagers. Eventually such behavior escalates to the point of digging tunnels in people's yards to hide out from who knows what. You've got to put your foot down now and nip it in the bud! Nip it, I say, and punish these boys before they do any more damage!"

At this point, the police officers bid a fond farewell and left Mom and our irate next-door neighbor to work things out. I guess they didn't share in the woman's dire predictions…or maybe prosecuting a three-and four-year-old was not judicially prudent.

"I apologize, madam," Mom said. "No excuses. The boys will clean up your deck immediately."

"Fine," replied the somewhat pacified, yet still indignant neighbor. "I'm hosting a gala this evening, and that deck better be spotless!" Then the woman stormed off in a huff.

My memory of what happened next is a little blurry. I remember Mom spraying Jimmy and me with a hose repeating the mantra, "Wait 'til your father gets home!" I don't remember how Jimmy and I got there, but I do remember being down on my hands and knees scrubbing the spotted pool deck with a toothbrush and soap. I don't know whether this was quite the punishment our disgruntled neighbor was looking for, but it sure steered me away from a career in dentistry.

TUNNEL TALE

It was the best of times and the worst of times: ah, those high school days. Sometimes those days were the best for me, yet the worst for someone else.

One such time took place in a sophisticated (yet not ostentatious) suburban community in southwest Chicago that shall remain nameless, because the town is crawling with lawyers. Living with my parents and I were my older brother, Jimmy, who was eighteen, and two younger brothers Mickey and Maury, ages sixteen and twelve. I was seventeen and a junior in high school at the time.

Across the street lived the two Marronie boys, Bruno and Rocky, each close in age to my younger brothers. The Marronie family had moved into the house across the street sixteen years ago, a week after we moved in. The two boys grew up with my family and were more like brothers than friends. We could quarrel among ourselves—even come to blows—but if someone from outside our little group tried to cross one of us, he or she had to face the whole lot of us. We were a close-knit group; sometimes we were united in friendship, and other times, we were united in power and intimidation.

To us, life was one big game to be won by us and lost by the other guys. Disrupting the peaceful, almost complacent lives of those around was just a part of this game—a part we really enjoyed. For instance, sometimes on Fourth of July, instead of just watching the festivities, we had our own, totally disregarding the fireworks ban (which we didn't agree with anyway). Our street would become a battlefield; bottle rockets, M-80s, and other explosive paraphernalia filled the air as a major battle between two teams of neighborhood kids raged. When the police finally arrived, the fun really began. We would spend the rest of the night running and hiding, lighting off more firecrackers, and then running and hiding again. We loved the thrill of the chase; it didn't occur to us that this guerrilla activity was dangerous and stupid. (Or maybe it did, but we didn't really care.)

We spent the cold winter season shoveling snow, building forts, and throwing snowballs at cars. Again, it was the thrill of the chase that warmed the cockles of our hearts.

Unfortunately, fall and spring seemed devoid of any such creative activities; there wasn't any snow to throw or fireworks to launch. We masqueraded as normal kids during these quiet months—and actually did some intellectual activities, like watching public television and reading books. (Sure, the books were about making bombs, but that still counted as literature to us.) We were particularly inspired by a PBS special on the original construction of the New York City subway. We watched every minute of the three-day miniseries as it explained the trench-and-cover method used to build the tunnel back in the late 1800s.

This method seemed ingeniously simple. It appeared that builders just dug a deep trench around New York City, then covered it with something strong enough to support tons of dirt piled on top of it. Eventually, streets would be built on top of that dirt, along with sidewalks and parking lots and various other urban structures commonly seen in a big city—"seen" being the key word. The tunnel itself wasn't seen at all, and this deception seemed devilishly simple.

It all began with a knock in the night and one scared teenager. The knock was on my front door at 11:00 PM one Saturday night, and the scared teenager was a local high-school kid who had just rolled his car across my front lawn.

"Uh…mind if I use your phone for a second? I uh…just wrecked my car," Ben Zinkowsky informed my older brother, who had answered the door.

"You what?! Are you OK?" Jimmy responded while rushing past Ben out the door onto the front porch, only to see an overturned car in the middle of our front yard, steam pouring from four wheels facing the sky.

"Hey, you got anything to eat?" Ben nonchalantly asked while strolling into the kitchen to make the call.

I think Ben called home, because there were several "yes, sir"s and "I don't know"s throughout the conversation. But Ben wasn't the only one making calls; flashing lights could be seen outside even before Ben hung up, accompanied by a loud knock on the door. Two police officers stood in the doorway, wanting to know whose car was lying in our front yard. Ben didn't try to hide anything; he walked right out the front door and into the waiting squad car.

Ben's father shortly arrived, and the two officers, Ben, and Mr. Zinkowsky all sat in the squad car, lights still flashing, for about an hour. The squad car then drove away with all of them in it. A tow truck came a couple of hours later to pull the wreck off to some junkyard before the sun came up.

The only remains of the incident were its mention in the Police Beat section of the local paper the next day—yet that write-up only said that Ben had received a traffic citation for speeding. It didn't say anything about the rolled car, or that the incident had happened in a residential part of town—where little kids and pets could and did wander about. It didn't say anything about the skid marks on Buckeye Street that showed that Ben must have been doing eighty miles per hour (the speed limit being twenty-five miles per hour) when he lost control of the car. The matter-of-fact nature of the story seemed to minimize the potentially deadly consequences of what very easily could have been a real tragedy.

Only a few months later, another potential tragedy threatened the safety of our neighborhood. It was Fourth of July weekend, and my brothers and I were playing "running bases" in the front yard, right where Ben's car had rolled end over end. Across the street, the Maronies were in their front yard, playing with Kala, their two-year-old niece. Kala went into the house around noon, and the neighbors walked across the street to join our game. We were all playing in front of my house, peacefully throwing the baseball, when a loud crash in the direction of the house across the street filled the air, and we witnessed a dark blue sedan rolling end over end across our neighbor's front yard. It rolled three times and ended up on lying on its roof—right where Kala had been playing only moments before!

We ran across the street just as two teenage boys crawled out of the shattered windows of the heaping wreck.

"Are you guys OK?" I asked as approaching police sirens filled the air.

"Yeah," said one boy, staggering to his feet.

"My dad's gonna kill me," mumbled the other.

"Kill you? Kill *you*? *You* almost killed *us*!" the elder neighbor, Bruno, emphatically protested. "My two-year-old niece was just playing right where *you* idiots rolled *your* car through *my* front yard. Thank God she went in for lunch, or she'd be dead!"

I couldn't say for sure that Kala would have been killed, but she definitely would have been injured. Bruno could get feisty at times, despite his average, adolescent stature I thought he was going to clock the guy who had expressed worry over his father's reaction, but luckily Bruno's little brother, Rocky, kept a tight grip on his brother's shoulders as sirens whined in the distance. Rocky was on the freshman football team and compared to Bruno, a bit of a gentle giant. While Rocky held Bruno, the two adolescent perpetrators feverishly tried to remove the beer cans from inside the car before the police got there, but we wouldn't let them.

"Those stay there," I said.

We weren't going to help these guys in any way; in fact, making things rougher for them seemed like a pretty good idea.

The police arrived mere moments later, and the two punks were whisked away in a squad car before a crowd of curious neighbors had a chance to form.

"That's the second car that's crashed in this neighborhood in the last six months," declared Bruno. "People drive around here like it's the Indy 500 or something. The cops can't be around all the time; there aren't enough of them. We've got to do something ourselves."

"Maybe we could get the city to put in speed bumps," I suggested.

"Nah, they won't do that. People would be afraid of hurting their precious cars," Bruno snidely commented. "I think this has to be an independent operation…grassroots organization and all that. If we wait for the city to do something, someone may get killed. If that idiot had crashed a few minutes earlier, Kala would be dead."

Just then, a shiny, compact, dark blue sports car came racing down the street.

"Hey, SLOW DOWN!" we all yelled together. It just whizzed by. Then another flashy sports car came racing right behind it.

"SLOW DOWN!" we yelled. It didn't. But this time, I picked up a football from the ground and threw it at the car. The ball sailed in a perfect spiral, and I had led the automobile just right. The ball hit the car with a loud thump as the speeding vehicle whizzed out of sight. A few minutes passed, and the same car came back down the street—this time driving quite slowly. It stopped in front of my house, and two teenage boys got out and walked up to the group of us. We all stood around nonchalantly, throwing the football.

"Who threw that ball?" one kid demanded.

"I did," I replied defiantly. "You drive like an idiot around here, and you may just get a football thrown at your car."

"Yeah, or something else…like a golf ball or a rock," chimed in Bruno. "This is our turf, and we're tired everybody using our neighborhood as some kind of racetrack. Now get back in your little sports car and go home," he added.

His abrupt tone may have been a little aggressive, but there were five of us and two of them. I think my friend was in the mood for a confrontation, but it didn't happen. The two speed demons just got in their car and drove away—slowly this time.

That afternoon, we got ahold of some black spray paint and made a sign on a big sheet of cardboard, then hammered it to a tree in the street median. The sign certainly looked homemade, but it was legible. It read,

SPEED LIMIT 25 MPH!!
VIOLATORS WILL BE SUBJECT TO:
FOOTBALLS, GOLF BALLS, TENNIS BALLS
MUD BALLS, ROCKS, AND WHATEVER

The part about the rocks was just for effect. Our intention was to scare people, not dent their cars.

The rest of the afternoon was quiet. We played football in my front yard. A couple of cars drove by, slowed down to read the sign, and drove away. Then, as twilight fell, a police squad car slowly prowled down the street and stopped by the sign. A tall, thin officer got out. He walked over to the sign, stopped to read it, and then shook his head and tore it off the tree.

"Who did this?" He yelled in our direction.

"Some kids," we yelled back. (We weren't lying; we just didn't say we were the kids. Information was given on a need-to-know basis, and the cops didn't need to know.)

On September 30, 1976, at 7:00 PM, the first shovelful of dirt was unearthed from my backyard, thus signifying the commencement of tunnel construction. There were initially three diggers: me, my youngest brother, and our irate neighbor who had vowed to rectify the traffic situation in our neighborhood. Looking back, I think it was more the adventure of digging that attracted Bruno and my little brother just dug because we told him to. We were older, and I think he was happy to partake in activities that involved older peers…plus, if he hadn't helped us, we'd have beaten him up.

The trench was dug in the southwest corner of my backyard and was about six feet deep, with plywood sheets countersunk twelve inches below ground level, covering the top. This setup was topped with twelve inches of mud and sod. The man-made cavern was about four feet deep and approximately thirty-one feet long—yet, from the outside, no one could tell there was a subterranean den of iniquity down there.

Even the tunnel entrance was undetectable to the casual observer. The entrance just so happened to be a doghouse with a false bottom that had hinges in the back. You could crawl in, push the floor down, dive into the tunnel, and then push the floor up behind you.

The only visible clue of the existence of the cavern was the emergency exit—a small hole in the south wall that penetrated all the way to the outside. This hole only had a diameter of about eight inches. It was only big enough for a kid to squeeze through in the event of a cave-in, and it was cleverly concealed by a prickly clump of overgrown thorn bushes.

We figured it was imperative that the tunnel's construction be a covert operation. My mom wouldn't have appreciated a thirty-one-foot trench in her backyard; besides, the whole idea was to build a secret hiding place we could use when being chased. Luckily, our digging began in September; darkness fell around 4:30 PM. We were able to come home from school on the four o' clock bus, then conduct our activities under the cloak of darkness. When Maury and I came in for dinner covered with mud, our mother was sheepishly informed that we were digging a humongous flower garden just for her. I don't know whether she bought that or just didn't want to know what we were really doing out there. My dad, on the other hand, wanted to know everything—but he usually got home from work around seven, and we had ceased digging by then. We usually didn't dig after dinner on school nights. If we did work after dinner, my parents were never surprised to find us missing; in fact, they seemed pleased that we weren't rotting our brains in front of the TV.

Bruno had a bit more difficulty escaping from home on school nights. They had rules over there like no TV after dinner and you had to either do homework or read a book. Bruno would hang a plastic bag in the shower so it sounded as if water were hitting his body. Then he would climb out the bathroom window, jump off the roof, and run over to our house. Rocky, who dug occasionally, would make the excuse that he had to go out to the garage to check the truck tires for leaks.

Day after day, we dug—working double shifts on weekends. Day after day, cars raced down the street in front of our house—twice as many on weekends.

The police had torn down our sign, but the police didn't seem to be stopping the speeders. It was only a matter of time before another moron rolled his or her car across my front lawn—and maybe this time, someone would get hurt. Digging the tunnel so we could throw stuff at speeding cars to force them to slow down almost seemed like a good idea. Our mission felt like one of social justice, with just a pinch of vigilante spirit thrown in.

The opening ceremonies for the tunnel were held on the evening of October 2, 1976. We didn't have any ribbon, so we used pink toilet paper permanently borrowed from the LaFemine boutique in town. (Our town had a lot of boutiques.) The tunnel opening was an auspicious event, complete with a bottle of Annie Greensprings wine to christen our project. The main diggers were all present: my brothers, my neighbors, and me. We made the positive decision that the tunnel would only be used as a place to hide after bombarding any motorists we deemed irresponsible or dangerous. In this sense, the tunnel became an instrument of social justice, not a plaything. We weren't allowed to goof off in it, and no girls were allowed inside the subterranean structure. The plan was to throw from the front yard, run around the side of the house into the backyard (where shadows would cover our escape), and then dive into the tunnel before anyone chasing us saw where we went.

That night, we decided to test out the tunnel's effectiveness. We positioned ourselves in the bushes along the front of our house. One strike force took the left flank, and I took the right. We waited, poised with tennis balls clenched tightly in each of our fists. The first target that drove down the street was a Cadillac that looked as if it belonged to one of the neighbors. The oldest daughter, a cheerleader, was driving, and the car wasn't moving too fast. We didn't bother attacking, because the girl behind the wheel would probably think throwing tennis balls at her car was some sort of adolescent flattery. This wasn't about teasing girls. Instead, we waited patiently, and a new opportunity emerged: a beat-up green sedan that was definitely driving too fast—not to mention blaring country music too loudly.

As the sedan cruised down the street in front of my house, it was bombarded by a barrage of tennis balls. *Boom, boom, boom*—I didn't see them hit, but I heard them. The repeating concussions sounded like Roman candles firing into the air, one after another. Despite the temptation to stay and watch the angry motorist, we wasted no time racing around the corner of the house into the safety of the shadows—and, in a matter of seconds, diving into the tunnel. The trapdoor was shut behind us before we first heard the driver's deep, angry voice.

"You little douche bags…I'm gonna kill you little bastards. You hear me, you little shits? Wherever you're hiding, I'm gonna find you, rip out your hearts, and stick them where the sun never shines!"

This sounded familiar. The tone, the diction, the reference to tearing out my heart and inserting it in a private orifice…it all meant only one thing: we had hit Big Red, and we'd better not get caught. This guy was nuts…not to mention big and mean. He had been kicked off the high-school football team for beating up a coach, and now his lifestyle involved smoking a fair amount of dope and drinking significant amounts of beer. The combination of probable inebriation, definite size, and obvious rage sent chills up and down my spine. It was pitch black inside the tunnel, and the only sound I could hear was that of my heart beating so fast and hard that I had to breathe through my mouth.

Clumps of dirt fell from the ceiling as Big Red stomped up and down on the ground above us like a two-year-old having a temper tantrum. I sure hoped the plywood below him was strong enough, or we'd all be in trouble. There was no turning back now—this had to work.

We silently sat in the dark cavern, not moving a muscle, for what seemed like hours…but I'm sure it was only a few minutes. Above, we could hear the clamoring footsteps of Big Red, stumbling in the dark, searching for us behind trees, in my mom's flower bed, and even inside the doghouse. We could hear his low, slurring voice mumbling some kind of psychotic mantra over and over again:

"I'm gonna kill those little bastards…they'd better not let me find their sorry asses. Kill little bastards. Kick sorry asses. Kill little bastards. Kick sorry asses…"

Luckily, Red never did find us. If he had, I probably wouldn't be writing this now. Looking back on it, I never was worried about him finding the tunnel, but I was afraid of him hearing our laughter.

After a while, it became clear that the tunnel was the perfect hideout, and Big Red wasn't going to find us. The ability to pummel cars with tennis balls and then disappear into a most excellent hideout made us feel like superheroes. Also, according to a sort of convoluted logic, we were using our superpowers for good by protecting our neighborhood…albeit in a slightly illegal, yet deviously creative manner.

First, Mickey started giggling, then Bruno, then Maury, and, before you knew it, sporadic bursts of muffled laughter were echoing throughout the tunnel.

The moon was high when we finally crawled out of the doghouse. The area around us had been silent for thirty minutes, and we were ready to ambush a new speeding motorist. I don't know what time it was, but it had to have been pretty late. There weren't any cars on the street in front of my house, and it was starting to get cold. I could easily squeeze the tennis ball in my palm as our assault team crouched in the bushes to await the next target.

It took about fifteen minutes, but finally another car driving too fast for our liking came down the street. In the moonlight, I could see a long, shimmering antenna glistening three or four feet above the car's rear wheel. *Must be a CB antenna*, I thought.

"Fire!" I yelled, and the ensuing barrage of tennis balls bombarded the bewildered motorist: *boom, boom, boom*. We were out of the bushes and sprinting into the shadows before we heard the first balls hit. Within moments, we reached the doghouse, popped the false floor open, and dove into the tunnel. Maury was the last one in; he raised the false bottom behind him, and we silently sat. Trickles of sweat dripped from my temples as we waited in the dank darkness to hear an irate motorist searching for us on the grounds above. Yet, we heard nothing. All was quiet, but we didn't dare move a muscle. Then, in the distance, the sound of approaching police sirens could be heard. Now the sweat was really rolling down my face, but I soundlessly held my position. It seemed as if an hour passed before we heard the first voice.

"No sign of the perpetrators over here…over."

The deliberate male voice seemed to be talking to someone else over some kind of walkie-talkie. We couldn't see who it was, and we certainly weren't going to blow our cover by popping our heads through the doghouse floor. I shimmied ever so carefully to the end of the tunnel, where I could peek out the small emergency exit. I couldn't see much, though, because of the bushes in front of my peephole. It looked as though whoever was looking for us was using a flashlight. I could see the contrasting beam of light waving from side to side, cutting through the darkness in a methodical pattern. The figure with the flashlight slowly walked closer to my tiny spy hole, and I caught a glimpse of something shimmering on the figure. It looked metallic…like keys or something. Then the figure spoke.

"All clear over here. Don't see a thing, over."

He was talking to someone on a walkie-talkie. I assumed it was a cop, and now my stomach felt as if it were doing back flips. My palms were sweating, but I stayed perfectly still, afraid to move even one muscle. From the tiny emergency exit, I could see the figure moving closer toward the bushes in front of me. Had he seen something? Why was he walking toward the bushes instead of back to the street?

Now the figure stood right in front of the bushes. I could only see his feet…and then I heard it: *ziiip*. A liquid spray hit the bushes right in front of me, and a little stream cascaded down the bush and trickled toward the emergency exit.

"Ahhh," moaned the voice. This was accompanied by another zipping sound as the little man-made river trickled down the emergency exit and into the tunnel. I heard leaves crunching as the person walked away.

"Aw, shit," I whispered, no longer too afraid to move a muscle. I scrambled to the other end of the tunnel.

There we sat in silence as a little ammonia-smelling puddle collected at our feet. Nothing filled our ears but silence; nothing filled our eyes but darkness; and nothing filled our noses but ammonia. After about a half hour, we surmised it was safe and climbed up from the doghouse floor. The street was quiet and empty, and it seemed as if there were a million stars in the pitch black sky. It was late—time to call it a night. Besides, it was a Friday night, and parents would be suspicious if we weren't home by eleven o'clock.

"Well," I said, stretching my arms over my head, "I've done enough damage for one day. Time for bed."

Bruno and Rocky, our partners in crime, quickly disappeared into the night as they walked across the street, and my brothers and I quietly crept in the back door. Sneaking up the stairs and into our bedrooms without being detected by my parents was fairly simple; Dad had already gone to bed, and Mom was watching TV on the back porch. I took off my muddy tennis shoes at the back door, so there would be no trace of the tunnel—and no unwanted questions from my mother the next day. Then I stealthily slipped up the stairs to my bedroom. Before I hopped in bed, I hung my muddy pants out the window and shook off the dirt. Now the deception was complete, and I could rest in peace.

The next morning at breakfast, the only thing Mom asked was whether my brother and I had seen the police car last night. Did we know anything about it?

"Uh…no, Mom, didn't see a thing," I innocently replied. "We were in the neighbor's basement all night, playing broomball."

Mom looked at me as if she didn't believe me, but then she walked away as if she didn't want to know what really happened. (Now that I'm a parent, I can understand this desire for blissful ignorance.) At any rate, nothing more was said, and I quietly poured a reservoir of syrup on my pancakes, devoured my breakfast, and rushed off to watch Saturday morning cartoons. (Sure, I was seventeen, but it was *Scooby-Doo*.)

That afternoon, while Mickey and I shot baskets in my driveway, it seemed as if the few cars that drove down the street were moving more slowly than normal. I stopped shooting and tried to catch a glimpse of the driver's face in the next car that went by. It was a man, and he appeared to be very focused: head straight, eyes on the road, both hands positioned perfectly on the steering wheel (at ten o'clock and two o'clock, respectively). It seemed as if he were looking for something—maybe a street to turn onto, maybe a small child running out into traffic…or maybe a tennis ball bombarding his windshield. It didn't really matter; he was driving slowly and paying attention. My neighbor, now shooting with us, attributed this driver's conscientious behavior to fear of retribution, rather than simple responsible behavior.

"Look at that guy," my neighbor said. "Now that's what I like to see! He must've heard about the tunnel. He's afraid."

"That's right, buddy…you'd better slow down!" he yelled at the car when it drifted nearly out of earshot.

Just then, a possibly familiar dark green sedan came barreling down the street. It was moving way too fast; I couldn't make out the driver.

"Hey! Slow down!" we all yelled together, but it didn't work. The car was already past our house when I threw the basketball at it. The ball didn't even come close, but Mickey still asked, in a brotherly (meaning totally blunt and insensitive) fashion, just what the hell I was doing.

"What are you going to do when someone gets out and starts chasing you?" he asked. "Run to the tunnel? What if he sees you go in the doghouse and never come out? Let's just suppose this guy isn't the brightest bulb in the closet…even so, he's probably watched *Hogan's Heroes* or *The Great Escape* or something like that before. You know, if he figures it out, the tunnel's history…and so are you."

"He's right," agreed Bruno. "We can't use the tunnel in the daylight, or someone'll find it."

"Agreed," I said. "We only attack at night, and we should probably only attack on weekends, not on school nights. That way, our parents won't get suspicious if we're not in bed by eleven o'clock."

We all agreed these were good rules. Keeping the tunnel secret was paramount.

Just to be safe, we refrained from using our secret weapon for the rest of that weekend.

Our next mission was a couple of weeks later, late one Saturday night in October. By then, the cool night air had turned into cold night air. Hiding in the bushes without moving was a real test of self-control, but the possibility of being seen by a passing motorist forced us to sit and shiver, with no movement to keep us warm. In a way, such aspects made our missions an exercise in building moral character and self-control…even though our intentions weren't quite so virtuous. After all, we were lying in wait to throw tennis balls at some unsuspecting individual who happened to be driving too fast.

It took awhile, but our chance came. Two cars seemed to be racing as they sped down the street, side-by-side. As they came within firing range, I heard Bruno's voice whispering, "Hold your fire, men, until you see the whites of their tires."

Now, I don't know if those cars even had whitewalls—it was impossible to see in the dark—but it sounded good.

Boom, boom, boom! We were off and running before the last concussion erupted. As I dropped through the doghouse floor, I caught a glimpse of three small lights and could hear excited male voices in the distance: "They went this way. C'mon, let's get those worthless little shits!"

By that time, the entire assault team was quietly concealed in the tunnel. We soon heard voices right on top of us. It sounded like three young males talking. I could tell they were young, because they used the F-word quite often—to describe every bush, tree, or shrub they thought we might be hiding behind. I concluded from the pitch of the voices that they were male, but that may have been presumptuous—they could have been three women with foul mouths and lead feet.

But then, the cry of alarm from one of the voices made it clear just who we were dealing with. It was Big Red.

"Hey…look at this f—ing grass. See how it's flattened down here? It looks like a f—ing footprint. Here's another one. Let's see where these go. Now I'll get those little bastards…hey, what the f—? They end. What'd those little shits do? Fly?"

"Maybe they was aliens, and they went up to their spaceship," another voice chimed in.

"They lead to the doghouse," Big Red commented. "How the f—could they fit in that thing?" Luckily, the possibility of a false bottom leading to an underground tunnel didn't occur to him. "This is f—ed. I'm outta here."

The sound of Big Red's footsteps crunching the grass let me know that they were walking around. I sat as still as possible for what seemed like an eternity. After a while, the subsequent silence seemed to indicate that they were gone. Yet we stayed in that tunnel, shivering and silent, for at least another half hour. By the time we climbed out, the stars were bright, and we could see our breath in the black night air. It was late; we called it a night and went home.

The next day was cold. Winter was coming fast. While discussing the previous night's escapades with Bruno, the idea of Big Red tracking our footsteps to the tunnel kept haunting me. I wondered how he had done that…but the answer was painfully apparent when I walked into the backyard and saw my footsteps imprinted in the slightly frozen grass. Our tracks from the street, around the house, and into the backyard were visible. The imprints were only slightly visible because of the bent grass, but with the coming snow, our footsteps would soon become even more apparent. Sooner or later, our fleeing footprints would lead our pursuers directly to the tunnel. Using the tunnel in the winter would be a problem.

To keep our secret safe, we decided to cease our covert tennis-ball attacks until the spring. Yet, we didn't abandon the tunnel. In fact, we conducted regular maintenance of our hole in the ground by scraping the walls. We even improved it by making it wider and digging little ledges in the walls where candles could light the inside.

Spring finally came, and the blanket of snow that covered the backyard melted. But the area around the doghouse was still quite muddy and most unpleasant. The inside of the tunnel was dry, but we had displaced a lot of dirt with our latest construction work, and the entrance was a mucky mess. Also, footprints in the mud were even more obvious than tracks in the frozen grass. We had to delay operations until things dried out.

Delaying our clandestine activities and maintaining a peaceful facade turned out to be a good idea, because our old neighbors behind us moved out, and new ones came in. Their backyard butted up against ours; only a six-foot wooden fence separated their property from our tunnel. This hadn't been a problem before; we hadn't really cared if the old neighbors were irritated by our activities. But the new family knew my parents. They even went to the same church as my family and my neighbor conspirators. We would have to keep the tunnel a secret from them—as well as from my parents, my neighbors' parents, the police, and basically anyone with any kind of authority. For a variety of reasons, it seemed prudent to hold off on our attacks on local traffic violators.

It was June before the ground back there was dry enough to prevent any obvious tracks. At the same time, the new neighbors began filling in their in-ground swimming pool in preparation for summer fun. The backyard pool was about a hundred yards from the fence separating their property from our tunnel.

Oddly enough, the pool preparation prompted the tunnel's demise. As he filled the pool, the pool man noticed a crack in the pool wall facing the fence. Upon further examination, the new owners discovered that the wall was actually bowing out—and, for some reason, the ground surrounding the pool was shifting. Well, I guess we hadn't kept the tunnel as good a secret as we thought, because, when the new neighbors mentioned the problem to my parents, my father had an idea of why the ground was shifting. He wasn't cognizant of our covert behavior; nonetheless, he knew about the tunnel and was impressed with our ingenuity.

There was no debate.

"You will fill in that tunnel immediately," he firmly stated.

Thus, what once had been an adolescent marvel of devious design became a laborious chore. Digging dirt because we wanted to had been fun. Digging dirt because we had to wasn't. Nevertheless, we persevered and filled it in.

Yet the memory of the tunnel didn't die. Some of the original diggers went on to become engineers, and my neighbor is still waging battle—only now, it's against life-threatening tumors, not life-threatening drivers.

B.O.W.

Throughout America, towns seem to revel in their high-school athletics—small towns, big towns, even suburban-wannabe towns. Preseason predictions about teams and players fill local newspapers. Sometimes, the evening news even runs a segment on up-and-coming athletes. Some may be interested out of nostalgia for their old glory days; others may view sports as a wholesome activity and enjoy seeing the youth of America participating in something that isn't illegal. Whatever the reason, people seem to pay attention to their town's high-school athletes, and every town has its share of local sports heroes.

America loves heroes, and local heroes help sell local newspapers. When I went to high school, my town had plenty of local sports celebrities, and many politically correct institutions—such as the local paper—reported on them regularly. Yet, my high school had plenty of members of another notable group—it just wasn't politically correct to discuss them in the newspaper. Therefore, their identities weren't well-known until we decided to make them well-known…or, at least, well-known within our school. This is the story about that certain type of celebrity and the adventure of creating public awareness.

It all began, like most good adventures, in a basement, underground, at night. It was a Sunday night in the September of my senior year in high school. We probably should have been doing homework, but instead, several classmates, my younger brothers (Mickey, a junior, and Maury, in eighth grade), and our next-door neighbors (Bruno and Rocky Marronie, who were about the same ages as my brothers), were shooting pool, watching TV, and perusing magazines full of pictures of naked women.

Bruno had provided this scandalous reading material. Then we had stashed the magazines in a cabinet in the back of the basement, where it was dank and musty, with cobwebs in the corners and water bugs crawling around clumps of dried dog doo on the floor. We figured my mom would never go back there.

As a matter of fact, my parents pretty much stayed out of the basement entirely. (Some things are better left unsaid; other things are better left unknown.) My brothers and I were responsible for the maintenance and upkeep of what was sort of a bachelor's paradise for teenagers. In accordance with adolescent standards of cleanliness, the place was a pigsty. The only semblance of tidiness could be found around the pool table, which got constant use. (Speaking of constant use, let's not forget the very comprehensive collection of nudie magazines from the sixties safely stored in the back cabinet.) However, the place was not totally devoid of any semblance of male sensitivity; Christmas lights hung year-round from the perimeter of the ceiling. Also adding to the festive ambiance of the basement was the bright silver garland that decorated the hot-water pipe running across the center of the ceiling.

In the midst of the festival of teenage iniquity taking place in this subterranean den, the starting fullback on the high-school football team opened the door and descended the short flight of stairs into the hallowed halls of Testosterone Central. A chorus of "DeMan! Ladies and gentlemen, here comes DeMan!" sprang up. (It was kind of like the *Cheers* cast greeting Norm.)

DeMan's real name was Nick Potowski, and he was a normal high school kid, who just happened to be built like a truck. Nick was a very easy-going guy who saved his aggression for the football field. DeMan's prominence on the gridiron, coupled with his relaxed demeanor, made him very popular at school and a bit of a celebrity in the basement.

"Hey man," one male voice loudly chimed in, "Player of the Week *again*…not bad!"

"Yeah, what is this now, three weeks in a row?" Someone piped up from behind his reading material in the rear of the basement.

"When is someone else gonna get it?" asked Maury.

"I don't know…maybe our high school doesn't have enough stars to fill in all the weeks," I quipped.

"I know one thing our school has plenty of," loudly proclaimed a voice from the pool table. "Bitchdom. We've got plenty of young apprentice bitches honing their skills to become totally screwed up feminist types."

One of the pool players then spoke in a very matter-of-fact tone: "Did you hear the latest? Brittany Purvis told Tommy Fitzgibbon that she'd go to homecoming with him…and then she said yes to Biff Prescott and dumped Tommy. I guess Tommy wasn't *popular* enough! What a bitch!"

"Yeah, we have more than our share of bitches in that school, that's for sure," commented one of the pool players.

"There's the understatement of the decade," chimed in Bruno. "You know what? We oughtta have a Bitch of the Week instead of a Player of the Week."

"Won't work," erupted a loud voice from behind some smut magazine in the back of the basement. "There are only fifty-two weeks in the year. Someone would be left out."

"All right, so we don't get *every* candidate in school," Bruno said thoughtfully. "We'll only name those chosen few who rise to levels of premier bitchdom…who go where no bitch has gone before. Kind of…the bitchiest of the bitchy." Bruno paused. "First we start with this Penis broad."

"That's Purvis," I corrected, then added, "Fitz is a good guy. That chick earned the title with that move. These broads need to be taught a lesson before it's too late. They think that with a pair of tits and a nice ass, they can just walk all over any guy."

"*This* broad can walk on me anytime," piped up the voice from behind a smut magazine in the back.

"It's our duty—not only to the other guys out there, but also the broads themselves." I lectured to anyone who was listening. "They need to learn about the real world now, so they won't waste any more time on any of that women's-lib bullshit."

"I never thought of it that way," Bruno agreed. "We *owe* it to each of those young ladies to kick their ass! Here's how we're gonna do it. First, we'll toilet paper the lucky winner's house. But this won't be just a regular TP job…it'll be a mega TP job, with three or four hundred rolls of toilet paper. We'll cover *every* tree in the broad's yard. Then…you know those bags of shredded paper the bank uses for printer tape and puts out on Thursday nights? We get a few of those and spread them all over her lawn…and then we apply the pièce de résistance: fresh horse manure—so fresh that it's steaming—all over the front porch. Without the manure, these broads would think it was just another TP job. They'd think it was cute. This isn't cute. We're making a statement here boys. We're talking about the future of our young people, damn it!"

"How you gonna move all this shit?" The monotone voice of supposed reason asked snidely from behind his reading material.

But Bruno was on a roll and responded immediately: "Rocky's on the freshman football team. We'll recruit his buddies. They'd love this. We can get maybe fifty guys. They'll be our infantry. We'll break 'em into platoons, and us guys here'll be the commanding officers. Most of those guys are little brothers anyway…they're used to taking orders and getting yelled at."

"You know, this just might work," commented one of the pool players. "We could use my Pinto as the command car, and put the rest of the infantry in pickups. Still, though…we need a central place to pick up the foot soldiers. It might look a little suspicious if fifty guys show up all at once at your house."

"I got it," Bruno piped up enthusiastically. "We'll tell 'em to wait in that alley by the ice-cream store downtown. Then, we just drive by with the pickups, and they all pile in. Simple."

That was that—everyone in the basement thought Bruno had an awesome idea. Yet, I don't think anyone took him seriously. The rest of the night played out like any ordinary night in the basement, with no more mention of the outrageous plan.

The rest of the week at school was pretty normal…except for the devious glint in Bruno's eye I saw every time I passed him in the halls. I wasn't sure anything was going to come out of Sunday night's bull session; I assumed we would leave it at juvenile ranting until he approached me in the cafeteria Thursday afternoon.

"We got the troops," he said. "They'll meet us in that alley downtown at 1900 hours on Friday. I think we can appropriate a case of TP from the school's janitor closet, and I'll take a bunch of guys to get the rest. I'm taking a special op's force after school to cruise Oden Avenue and rip off every john in every restaurant for twenty miles, and you know that's a shit-load of toilets. Also, we're having a chalk talk in the basement tonight at 1800 hours. I'll bring the blackboard. You bring the chalk."

Nothing else was said.

That night I was watching *Barney Miller* in the basement when Bruno, chalkboard in hand, came bounding down the stairs from the garage.

"How'd you get out? Aren't you supposed to be studying?" I asked.

"Oh, you know…the old hanging-bag in the shower routine never fails" he nonchalantly replied, thrusting the blackboard in my face. "Gimme the chalk."

In just a few moments, a house and some squiggly things that resembled trees were sketched out on the board. My neighbor then assumed the posture of a college professor, put the chalkboard on an easel (I think it was his little sister's) and started pointing and lecturing as if this were halftime in the locker room at the Bears game.

"Here's the house…with trees here, here, and here. This one's a big elm. It'll take one, maybe two hundred rolls by itself. We attack from the side, use the neighbor's bushes for cover, and unload our troops from the street right in front of the house next door. I'll take some of Rocky's buddies and hide the supplies in these tall bushes over here before the troops get there. We'll get the TP and printer tape there about 1700 hours, after it's dark. You're in charge of the horse manure. We can use my pickup to get it after school tomorrow from Keystone Stables. We'll need about two hundred pounds of the really smelly shit. We won't stash it in the bushes with the other stuff—we'll bring it with us when it's mission time. That way, we know the shit's fresh.

"We'll have to be fast," Bruno continued, "and finish the job before the cops come. If they barricade that street before we get out, we're up shit creek without a plunger…Maybe we should post a lookout at the corner."

"Naw…why waste a man on watching traffic when he could be throwing toilet paper?" I reasoned. "We'll hear the cops if they come, and most of these guys are smart enough to get away on their own. If they aren't, well…we don't really want them anyway."

"Yeah, but what if they squeal? My mother would kill me!" Bruno's concerned tone was uncharacteristic of him.

"That's why we have a code of silence," I replied. "We tell the infantry soldiers that there is to be a code of silence, and if anyone is captured, nobody says *nothin'* to nobody. If they do, the rest of the guys are obligated to beat the crap out of him."

"They'll buy that," Bruno confidently affirmed and immediately resumed strategizing the escapade. "We'll meet here at 1800 hours Friday. Have all the platoon commanders present. We'll brief 'em, and I'll get the infantry downtown in the alley. We'll pick 'em up at 1900 hours and go directly to Barnes Field for warm-ups. Then we'll break our men into their different units, load the transport vehicles, and proceed to the Purvis house. We'll unload in the street, grab the stuff out of the bushes, hit, and be out of there in ten minutes. Get it?"

"Got it," I replied.

"Good. See you tomorrow at 1800 hours," responded Bruno as he confidently picked up his chalkboard and went home.

The next day seemed like a typical Friday. The football guys wore their letter sweaters to school, and the cheerleaders dressed up in their little skirts and rah-rah sweaters. Word spread throughout the BOW high command to meet at my house at the previously designated hour, and I went with Bruno to the stables right after school.

The wranglers at the stables were happy to let us fill four garbage bags (double bagged for extra strength) with what they said was their finest shit. The sun was still up, so we couldn't see the steam. However, one whiff from any bag confirmed that this was the good stuff.

We proceeded to my house, left the manure in the garage, and parted company. Bruno would handle stashing the rest of the munitions in the bushes next to Purvis's house.

The adventure had begun. Now we just had to get to 1800 hours without my mom or Bruno's mom suspecting we were up to anything abnormal (well…more abnormal than usual).

When 1800 hours finally arrived, I was in the basement. The plan proceeded like clockwork, seemingly of its own momentum. The four platoon commanders (the very same classmates who had helped concoct this scheme the previous Sunday night) and Bruno all bounded loudly down the stairs into the basement at approximately the same time. Bruno put the chalkboard where it had been the night before, then directed the platoon commanders to focus their attention toward it. Bruno briefed them on the plan, showed them where he had stashed the TP and printer tape, and explained that we were going to get in our vehicles, drive slowly by the alley near the ice-cream shop downtown, and pick up the infantry.

In a calm and very simplistic manner, he explained, "They can just dive in the backs of the pickups as we roll by. It has to be quick. The police station is only a couple blocks away, and they might be a little suspicious if they see thirty guys come running out of some alley and dive into a couple of pickups. So we have to be discreet…drive casual. Once we get everybody, we'll get the hell out of there and go to Barnes Field. We'll empty out the trucks and have the foot soldiers warm up as a group with some preBOW calisthenics."

"What's BOW?" I asked.

Without hesitation, Bruno replied, "Bitch of the Week."

Obviously he'd already thought about this quite a bit, and I was interested in seeing how the rest turned out. I shut my trap as he continued.

"After about forty-five minutes, we'll get the infantry together and assign them to platoons; you guys are the four platoon commanders. You got ten minutes once we pull up in front of Purvis's place to cover each of these trees with toilet paper and spread the shredded printer tape all over the front lawn. The munitions will be in these bushes." Bruno tapped the chalkboard. "Also, we'll have a special-operations force in charge of the horse manure." That was my job. "They'll spread it all over the front porch. That will be tricky, because there's a ceiling light on the porch. We'll have to be quick."

"Why don't we just shoot it out with a BB gun?" queried one of the platoon commanders.

"No!" I emphatically answered. "No vandalism."

"What do you mean, no vandalism? This isn't vandalism?" questioned another morally conscious platoon commander.

"No, it's not," I calmly explained. "Vandalism is when you wreck something that is already there. We're not wrecking anything that's already there. We're just adding a few things."

I doubt if he agreed with me, but it didn't really matter; these guys were committed to the adventure no matter what. We all quickly left the basement and mounted our vehicles for the next phase.

One of the platoon commanders led the caravan of two pickups and two cars as we slowly rolled in front of the appointed alley; I rode shotgun in that same command car. I turned around in the passenger seat to an extraordinary sight—it resembled that scene in *Oliver* where all the little kids fill the street. What seemed like a thousand foot soldiers ran from behind the shadows of the alley and hurled their bodies into the beds of the pickups. From there, it was on to Barnes Field, where the thirty or so infantry soldiers (it only seemed like a thousand) were herded to the middle of the park for calisthenics. Bruno lead the infantry as they obediently practiced some sort of arm and shoulder gyrations that were supposed to simulate throwing a roll of toilet paper into a tree. They also did some running in place and sit-ups with the subordinate enthusiasm you'd expect from a bunch of little brothers.

When warm-ups were finished, we herded the infantry into one big group, and platoon assignments were given out. Each platoon commander then had five minutes to take his group aside and explain the platoon assignment—for instance, which tree or bush to hit. Everybody then got back together in one big group for the announcement of the lucky BOW winner and the declaration of the code of silence. As I suspected, everyone thought the code was a great idea—I think some guys actually hoped they would get a chance to beat on certain individuals.

The pickups followed the green command car to the target in silence. There, we quickly unloaded and ran into the bushes to secure the munitions. In moments, the attack began.

Rolls of toilet paper flew through the air while brown garbage bags of printer tape were emptied and spread all over the neatly manicured lawn. Seven minutes later, the first stage of action was nearly complete. I noticed Mickey and two infantry soldiers on the roof, decorating the television antenna with TP. I had no idea how they got up there, but it didn't really matter; the roof contingent seemed like a good idea.

The last phase involved the horse manure. Two infantry-men quickly brought the bags up from the rear, and we doused the front porch with a one-inch layer of the steamy, smelly stuff. Within ten minutes, the mission was complete. We climbed back into our vehicles and got out of there.

As we left, I felt a few drops of rain falling from the dark sky above. The weatherman had predicted rain, but we'd lucked out—thus far.

By the time we got to my house and unloaded the personnel, it was a full-fledged downpour. Luckily the infantry soldiers would only have to walk a couple blocks to get their bikes downtown. It was probably about 2100 hours—close to the infantry's bedtime. Their game would be early the next morning. The platoon commanders and the rest of the high command didn't have to get up early, so we went down into the basement to shoot pool, peruse dirty magazines, and revel in our glory.

"Man, we got outta there just in time!" Bruno enthusiastically exclaimed. "I was in the last pickup, and I could see the cop's cherries stop at the Purvis joint just as we turned the corner. No casualties, though…they didn't chase us."

"That's too close. I didn't even know the cops were on their way. That rain's gonna make that roof job one royal mess," I said ruefully. "All the other stuff will just be a pain to pick up tomorrow, but the wet toilet paper on the roof will bleed into the shingles. It shouldn't wreck anything, but they'll have racing stripes. I guess that qualifies as vandalism…Well, gentlemen, now we can't get caught. If we ever do this again, we're gonna have to be extremely careful."

"What do you mean, ever do this again?" Bruno emphatically questioned. "This has been a huge success! No casualties, a helluva TP job—the best this town's ever seen—and there's enough prospects to have a BOW every week for the next ten years."

"Or until you idiots graduate…whichever comes first!" shouted a wry voice from the back of the room, behind some reading material.

"How do you know we could get the manpower again…not to mention the toilet paper?" I asked. "We probably cleaned out every restaurant on Oden Avenue."

"Don't worry about the manpower. I'll get Rocky's buddies, and the bank leaves a new batch of printer tape out every week—sometimes on Wednesdays, sometimes Thursdays. The manure is no problem—horses gotta shit. We can get the toilet paper from the storage room at the high school—the one in the basement, behind the towel room, underneath that big clock…where they store the pole-vault pit. No one goes in there…well, almost no one." Bruno spoke in a confident tone, as if these were plans, not ideas.

The rest of the night was pretty routine: shooting pool, looking at dirty magazines, and spitting tobacco juice into plastic cups. In the end, everybody went home at about 2200 hours, after watching *Magnum PI*; some guys had the varsity football game the next afternoon.

The varsity game was in a neighboring suburb. The gloomy skies were spitting sprinkles—just teasing before the big downpour. Not many people made the trip besides the parents and the cheerleaders. Bruno and I went with my dad to watch Mikey and our friends. My dad observed that the weather was tailor-made for DeMan, and he was right. DeMan carried the ball for a couple of big gainers and a touchdown. I was pretty sure by the end of the day that he would get Player of the Week…again. However, the real question was, who would be crowned Bitch of the Week?

Some of the talk at school Monday centered on the game, but most of the conversation within my social sphere involved the awesome TP job on Purvis's house. Most of the boys were excited and totally supported the BOW escapade. Some of the girls were appalled and called it an immature act by a few jerks. Other girls, mostly the ones who weren't afraid they were next, thought it was outrageous, but probably deserved. At any rate, most of the popular chicks (cheerleaders and the like) gave me the cold shoulder…but that wasn't really anything new. These socially acceptable individuals didn't really associate with my type anyway. Yet, I wondered if BOW had the sustainable support necessary to continue. Were the leaders of BOW going to continue to risk being ostracized by this cadre of supremely mature, socially acceptable, and popular broads? That question was quickly answered.

"I got the plan!" Bruno excitedly told me Monday night. "We hold an election in the cafeteria on Thursday during lunch to vote for the newest BOW. That way, more people get involved. Anyone can vote for a quarter…and for a buck, they can nominate their own candidate. But it can't be just any old bitch. They can only take broads from the junior and senior classes." In response to my questioning gaze, Bruno explained, "Girls don't reach full bitchhood until sixteen or seventeen; until then, they're just moody. Anyway, we then use the money for supplies. We still hit the bank for the printer tape and stables for the shit, but this way, we don't have to go up and down Oden Avenue to get the TP. Plus, we can always hit the janitor closet if we come up a little short."

"Sounds good," I commented, with thoughtful respect for this guy's clandestine creativity. "I especially like the voting idea—makes BOW look democratic, like we're enforcing the will of the people, not just randomly dumping horseshit on some broad's front porch. The only problem is that I'm not going to be around this weekend. I'm leaving Saturday morning to visit some college. You'll have to run this one without me."

"No problem," responded Bruno. "Piece of cake."

Thursday rolled around rather quickly. As promised, Bruno set up the polls at a center table in the school cafeteria with a shoebox and a sign that said BOW Voting. There was a pretty long line there too, with plenty of diversity: boys and girls, nerds and jocks, greasers and gearheads all waited to cast their vote. No socially acceptable debutantes waited with them—probably because their own names were on the ballot.

As long as no one threw food or started a fight, the cafeteria cops left us alone.

Just as he had the week before, Bruno clamored down the stairs into the basement on Thursday night, chalkboard in hand, to strategize our next adventure.

"This is gonna be a tough one," he stated. His tone was deadly serious, as if he were plotting out brain surgery, not a TP job. "The target's on a cul-de-sac in that new development on Lashea Lane. There's only one way in and one way out. If the cops block that entrance, we're dead. I've mapped out her house."

Bruno showed me the chalkboard and pulled out one of those retractable pointers to elaborate. "We've got trees here, here, and here. We can stash the munitions in these bushes, and there's a fence that runs across the entire backyard and separates their property from Killarny Lashea Park. You see, the park butts up *directly* to their backyard! There's our in. We unload the infantry in the park's parking lot, just off Killarny Street, a mile from the entrance. Then we double-time it across the park to attack from the rear. I'll get the munitions in the bushes beforehand, and we'll be outta there before she even knows what hit her."

"One problem," I commented. "How do you get thirty guys, in the dark, over—in a reasonable amount of time, mind you—a cyclone fence that's what, seven feet high…with sharp metal points sticking up at the top?"

Again, with a spontaneity that demonstrated his creative, yet devious genius, Bruno instantly had the answer.

"We'll steal those big floor mats they have in the entrance of the high school and throw those over the top. Then the troops can just climb the fence and belly roll over the top, like Marines. We leave the mats there and do the same thing on our way out."

Any doubt that the execution of this BOW would be conducted with the utmost in systematic delinquency was erased. The mission was in good hands—demented, but good.

Bruno and I went to the stables right after school on Friday, filled our bags with the freshest manure we could find, and went back to my house. I then left town with an alumnus of the college I was visiting. As we drove away, I looked at the trees and reflected on how some things would just happen, no matter what I did. For instance, fall would end; winter would come. I would have to shovel the driveway. Horses would always make manure, people would always need toilet paper…and there would be a BOW that night. Bruno was in command, and whatever happened, happened. It wasn't my responsibility if they got caught; I hadn't gotten them into this. They chose to do it. I further rationalized myself into delusions of irresponsible bliss, then settled in for the five-hour drive.

It was late Sunday night when I finally got home—too late to call and get the lowdown on how things had gone with BOW. But I heard about it soon enough. In the cafeteria Monday, Bruno informed me that the operation had been a humongous success; however, the troops had barely gotten away. Apparently the police had arrived just as the infantry was finishing; squad cars had blocked the entrance to the housing development on Lashea Lane. Luckily, the authorities hadn't anticipated an attack from the park, so the troops had just rolled over the fence, run to the pickups, and gotten the hell out of there.

However, it was now painfully obvious that future attacks would require a more devious strategy to evade the cops.

"We can't count on every BOW to have a park in their backyard. There're too many broads," Bruno thoughtfully observed.

"Yes, I concur, my deviant friend," I commented. "We don't want to deny any deserving candidate the opportunity to be crowned. That would be bitch bias and definitely discriminatory. Still, though…we've gotta find a way to deploy the troops, hit, and get out of there before the coppers block our escape. We've gotta do something…but what?"

The answer came Wednesday night. as Bruno bounded down the stairs into the basement, excitedly proclaiming that he'd solved the problem.

"I've got it!" he said. "One of the infantry boys got their hands on a police scanner. We can listen to the cops and know where they're going. We can hit and be gone before they get too close."

"That might just be the ticket," I said. "Now we'll show those broads who can be sophisticated...technically sophisticated, that is. This is gonna be great!"

The rest of the week at school went pretty much as usual. There was some talk about BOW, but most of the high-school gossip centered around who was dating whom, who dumped whom, how the football team had played the Saturday before, and girls' failure to understand how immature some boys were. Neither of the previous BOW winners would talk to me when passing in the hall...but, as I've said before, that really wasn't anything new. However, some of the other girls who did talk to me wanted to know who was going to get it next. I think they felt sadistic delight at the notion that the whole election was a sham, and our troops were really just targeting debutantes we weren't especially fond of, but couldn't speak out against for political reasons. I assured them that nothing could be further from the truth—but to no avail. They were going to believe what they wanted to believe. I realized just how important it was to keep an open mind and avoid making this a popularity—or, I should say, unpopularity—contest.

I was genuinely excited when Thursday rolled around and students began the democratic process. They cast their votes to decide just whose front porch would meet manure that Friday night.

Bruno and I had the usual chalk talk Thursday night, outlining our strategy and planning escape routes. The lucky winner was some broad who lived only about a mile away, and we knew our way around all the streets and most of the backyards between our command center and the target. With the police scanner, we thought we were invincible. We even got so bold as to institute the roof patrol—a special detachment that would precede the ground forces on every mission to TP the chimney and TV antenna. This was a dangerous assignment, but Mikey, who'd invented the maneuver, volunteered to lead the assault and got two volunteers from the infantry.

Friday night came, and, as scheduled, the munitions were in place, and the platoon commanders' meeting included two new officers (classmates) who manned the police scanner and served as lookouts. They would position themselves at the entrance, about a half mile from the BOW target, and monitor the airwaves to assess police movements during our attack. They were to gauge when the cops were too close and it was time to abort the mission. These two guys were perfect for the assignment. One was quarterback on the football team, so we figured he was good at making snap decisions. The other guy was a back—trained in getting the hell out of there. He knew when to run.

Another addition to the adventure was a full-length Army coat that a classmate loaned me for the occasion. His girlfriend wouldn't let him participate, so he offered the gear as a covert gesture of support. The guy wasn't stupid—just whipped.

In addition to the coat, I wore my dad's WWII Army helmet on my head and a cigar in my mouth—which I lit as the command car pulled out of my driveway. As the command car led the procession of pickups slowly past the ice-cream store and off to Barnes Field, I was struck by the unbridled enthusiasm of the infantry troops streaming out of the alley and hopping into pickups. Some guys probably got involved because they believed in the cause—whatever that was—and others joined simply for the opportunity to raise hell with their buddies. Whatever the reason behind it, it was clear their enthusiasm made these operations possible.

Once we arrived at Barnes Field, the troops proceeded in an orderly fashion to line up in rows of eight and do calisthenics. The platoon commanders hovered around the perimeter of the infantry troops, barking out motivational comments like "Suck in that gut, mister. Pump those legs! My grandmother can lift her knees higher than you!"

I don't think the platoon commanders were really mad at anyone; it was just part of the drama. After the brief warm-up, we all got together in a big huddle. The lucky winner was announced, and a chorus of cheers accompanied the proclamation.

Most of those guys probably didn't even know that girl, but I still heard comments like, "Oh yeah, she's a bitch. She should get it. We're doing this town a favor giving it to that broad. They should be thanking us."

Within minutes, we piled into our vehicles and proceeded to the extraction point. Bruno and I had decided to launch the assault about a block south of the target to ensure a clean getaway. The problem was that, as had been the case with our second caper, this BOW lived in a development, and there were only two ways to get in or out. These arteries could easily be blocked by a couple of squad cars. According to our crude traffic study (made by talking to some kids at a lemonade stand), we had determined that the south entrance had the least traffic, so we unloaded there. The lookout car parked at the northern entrance, its occupants scanning the police channels. They would alert us at the first sign of trouble.

The roof patrol went first as the troops piled out of the vehicles and stealthily advanced toward the target. Before we got to the BOW's front lawn, the roof patrol was already out of sight. They must have been behind the house, finding a way to get up there. It was at this point that the green Charger came barreling down the street, blaring its horn.

"Abort! Abort! They're coming. Abort the mission!" the two lookouts screamed as the car whizzed by honking its horn.

Immediately I screamed, "FALL BACK! Everyone, fall back! Grab the stuff out of the bushes and double-time back to the trucks!"

I thought of the roof patrol, but there was no way to get word to them. They were big boys; they knew the risks. Sometimes the needs of a few were outweighed by the needs of many—and we needed to get out of there! We got back to the trucks and took off. I didn't hear any sirens as we left, but we got out of there pretty quick and went to the only place we knew to go: my house.

It must have been a sight: two pickup trucks and two cars pulling into my driveway and about thirty guys all piling out from the truck beds. My mom was standing on the front porch, arms crossed across her chest, when I got out of the command car.

"Well, what's up, General?" my mother snidely inquired, seeing me in my Army helmet and coat.

"Aw, Mom!" I exclaimed. "We're just playing capture the flag. Nothing's up."

I don't know if she believed me. She probably didn't, but just grunted an "Uh huh, sure," and went inside. Meanwhile, teenage boys were scrambling out of pickups parked in the driveway and running across my front yard, headed whichever way was home. Most of the infantry had a game early the next morning; this BOW had been a bust, so there wasn't any good reason to break curfew this time. The remaining high command proceeded to the basement for debriefing and to play a few games of pool.

Platoon commanders reported that we had no casualties among the infantry. The cops hadn't caught anyone on the ground…but the roof patrol—Mickey and two loyal infantry soldiers—was still out there. If they got caught and squealed, my mom would find out we weren't playing capture the flag. I'd be in big trouble for lying—not to mention attempting to dump two garbage bags of horse manure on someone's front porch. Yet, we couldn't go back to the scene of the almost-crime to try to rescue them; the coppers would get us for sure. The prudent plan was to stay put and just wait.

I was conjuring possible lies I could tell my parents, just in case, when Mickey and his two cohorts clomped down the basement stairs with a story to tell.

"We were on the roof and saw you guys leave seconds before the cops came," Mickey excitedly proclaimed. "We just froze and hoped they wouldn't see us. They had *two* squad cars and even a dog. Lucky thing we were up there, or that mutt would've smelled us. They searched all over the place—in the bushes, around the trees, even in the garbage can. Luckily they never looked up, and we kept perfectly quiet…except when I ripped one, but I guess they mistook that for a bullfrog. We climbed down about a half hour after they left. It was a close one!"

"Anyone caught?" inquired Bruno.

"We're all here, aren't we?" my brother replied.

The rest of us whiled away the remainder of the evening performing the regular basement rituals of chewing tobacco, reading smut magazines, and playing pool. With no casualties, plenty of toilet paper and printer tape left, and two garbage bags of fresh horse manure salvaged from the narrow escape, BOW would live to grace another day, I surmised.

On Monday, the aborted target tried to give her girlfriends at school the impression that the BOW brigade's efforts had been foiled, never to return again. Her side of the story implied that failure had been the inevitable outcome of this testosterone-driven endeavor, since the female gender was simply superior. She was right about two things: we did lose the battle, and we did have testosterone. However, BOW wasn't over, and we were determined to win the war. Also, thanks to our latest aspiring young feminist, the importance of BOW was made crystal clear, and the assertion that an additional X chromosome and a little estrogen made anyone superior was typical female bullshit. You could feel the electricity among the male students the rest of the week. BOW couldn't die; it was needed. Yet, I knew BOW couldn't continue without measures to keep us out of jail. Our last escapade had been too close.

The answer came in the form of a wrench—and a plan concocted by two devious minds, with a little help from television drama. Word had gotten back to Bruno that one of the infantry soldiers had a special kind of wrench normally used by fire departments to open hydrants. A lot of water came out of those things; I knew their unauthorized activation usually involved at least one cop car…maybe two. Our plan was to take a special-operations force across town from the target location and have them use the wrench to open not one, but two or three fire hydrants. The goal was to divert as many cops as possible away from the BOW target long enough to christen the house and get the troops out of there. The plan seemed simple, yet delightfully devious. I was convinced it would work, and BOW was alive and well.

The normalcy of the rest of the week disguised our plan to execute BOW, complete with the diversionary tactic, on that Friday night. However, I was surprised Thursday afternoon when the usual BOW ballot box was absent in the cafeteria. It was my impression that the plan was on—but we needed a lucky winner. Bruno explained to me in the cafeteria that the target had already been unanimously chosen by the infantry troops.

"One of the boys had a party last weekend when his parents were out of town, and his mom got a call from a certain mother tattling on him. All the guys are pissed…and they think she deserves this week's award," stated Bruno in a matter-of-fact tone.

"A mother!" I exclaimed. "What are you, nuts? We can't get a mother. Broads from school are one thing…but not a *mother!*"

"I know. I know. But this is supposed to be a democratic process," Bruno argued. "And we owe it to these guys. Also, we're gonna need them if BOW is gonna keep going at all."

I thought about how integral the infantry soldiers had been to BOW—how they had obeyed orders without question and risked capture, all to christen some unsuspecting broad—who wasn't even in their class. Yes, these guys had earned their own adventure, and we did need them. Bruno had a good case, I supposed, even though I thought BOW was maybe crossing the line. Yet, I was a victim of circumstances; I had to agree.

There was no talk Thursday afternoon at school about BOW or who the lucky winner might be; with no elections in the cafeteria, most students thought the weekly coronation was over. However, just like clockwork, Bruno showed up in my basement that evening, chalkboard in hand. He hadn't named names before, and I was a little surprised when he identified the target. Not only was the BOW a mom, but she was also a neighbor! (*Oh, well,* I thought. *Let's just see how far this line bends.*)

The logistics seemed simple enough, given our familiarity with the area and the three or four escape routes available to cars and trucks—not to mention the backyards and bushes available to anyone on foot. However, we didn't really expect the police to show up in time anyway, because we'd taken our delinquency to the next level with our fire-hydrant plan. Synchronizing the attack with a diversionary misdemeanor should draw law-enforcement attention away from the target.

We decided we needed fresh manure, and it seemed especially pungent when Bruno and I strolled through the stables Friday afternoon. The platoon commanders arrived at my house at the appointed hour that evening. However, instead of going to Barnes Field after picking up the foot soldiers, we went to a sort of community clubhouse at another park to organize the troops. After everyone had their assignments, one of the platoon commanders requested a team prayer, like before a football game. However, I put the kibosh on that, saying it would be making light of God, and there are some things you just didn't mess around with. A few other members of the high command agreed, and we proceeded with what we thought was a modicum of scruples intact.

The clubhouse wasn't far from the target site, and at the previously designated time, the pickups and cars pulled in front of the pristine two-story colonial. Whoops and hollers made an impromptu battle cry, and we attacked. Apparently the lucky winner wasn't home; the infantry soldiers didn't even try to be quiet. They chatted among themselves as they threw TP in the majestic, old elm trees, printer tape on the finely manicured lawn and christened the freshly painted porch with horse manure in record time.

We were just about to leave when I noticed a couple of the infantry huddled over the driveway, applying what appeared to be black tape to the concrete. They were taping "BOW" on the ground as a sort of calling card. I didn't think this was really necessary, but merely adding stuff didn't fit my definition of vandalism. Therefore, I deemed it OK.

Back at my house, the troops leaped off the trucks and scattered. The commanders retreated to my basement to critique the evening and revel in their juvenile glory. The sentries that had monitored the police scanner reported that the diversion had worked, and three cop cars had been dispatched to the other side of town just as we began the attack. With the scanner and hydrant wrench, we now could confidently evade the cops, and we felt pretty clever. The future for BOW seemed to shine like a starry, starry night.

However, if every dark cloud has a silver lining, it figures that every silver lining comes with a dark cloud. A dark cloud seemed to be hovering around Bruno when I saw him Monday at school.

"I gotta quit BOW," he explained softly in a resigned monotone as he stared at the ground. "My mom got a call from Friday night's lucky winner and got really pissed. My mom said I have to quit…'or else.'"

"Or else what?" I asked.

"Don't worry about that," fervently replied Bruno. "I'm out. It's over. There are some things you just don't screw around with, and this is one of them."

"So you're just gonna quit…just like that?" I asked. "What about all those prospective candidates? What about teaching these broads a lesson? The same bitchy mistreatment that happened to Fitz could happen next year, or the year after that. This town needs us…even though they don't know it yet."

"You may be right," my neighbor explained. "But I gotta take care of myself. I'm out. Let the bitches run free and learn the hard way, like the rest of us. This is my final decision."

The loss of Bruno was a death blow to the entire operation. He wasn't the only brain behind the operation, but his was certainly the most devious and enthusiastic. Also, he had organized all the infantry soldiers and munitions acquisition. One could say he was the human-resource manager and purchasing manager, all rolled into one.

After our discussion, it was obvious the operation was over. There was no way I was going to try to pull BOW off by myself. Plenty of porches would never see the spread of horse manure, but the memory would live. I figured that as long as there were broads who needed to be taught a lesson—and knuckleheads like us to teach it—the spirit of BOW would survive somewhere...maybe in some kid's basement.

LINKSTERS ON THE BOULEVARD

Golf is supposedly a gentleman's sport, played by sophisticated individuals. Why chasing a little white ball and hitting it with a stick is considered sophisticated, I don't know, but in an effort to acquire some sort of social status, the boys in my neighborhood decided to pick up the game. We thought we could somehow diffuse our rather unflattering reputation as unruly teenagers. (I can't imagine where such a reputation originated; innocent angels that we were, we had merely been digging tunnels and nominating BOWs.)

This is a story about fitting a square peg in a round hole...or rather, fitting nine holes with a bunch of square pegs.

A few of those square pegs were my younger brothers Mickey and Maury, alumni of the BOW and tunnel projects, along with my neighbor Bruno and his younger brother, Rocky—also distinguished members of these socially unacceptable escapades. Also included in this golf adventure were a few other characters from the neighborhood who had tarnished their reputations by complying with these escapades. The tunnel and BOW were now years in the past, but such escapades remained ever present in the memories of the silver-haired crowd in town. All of us were older now and had successfully graduated high school, then gone to college instead of prison—without flunking out, no less. In fact, I was in my third year, Mikey his second year, and—in defiance of all the odds—Bruno had overcome cancer and was studying to be a doctor. Yet, the stigma of our past still loomed, causing many townsfolk to perceive us more as nonconformist dirtbags than as mature, responsible students. We all decided that since we were supposed to be evolving and gaining public respect, we should at least appear to be doing socially acceptable stuff—like playing golf.

However, playing on a regular, preexisting golf course didn't seem to embrace the true ambiance of the game. We wanted to be like those old-time golfers in the pictures at my dad's golf club. He said those men, who hailed from Scotland, had invented golf in their home country and then brought the game to America. According to Dad, in the olden days, men used to just walk out their front doors with a flask of whiskey and a club, then meander over hills, through fields, and over streams, whacking that little white ball. Some holes, he said, were as much as a par twenty-nine; the men would start in the morning and be away from the house all day while the womenfolk tended to the children and made dinner.

The olden days sounded pretty good, and we decided to emulate these pioneers of the game by creating our own course, which meandered throughout our quiet, residential neighborhood in suburban Chicago. Back in that day, fields and streams had linked together, thus forming a natural links course; we decided to design our own similar links course. Sure, we didn't have fields and streams, but we compensated with sewers and sidewalks linked together by parkways and front yards. We used actual golf balls, but limited the club selection to nine and eight irons, so as to avoid breaking any windows unnecessarily. The idea that people would resent our making divots and launching little white missiles from their front yards seemed preposterous; we weren't really *wrecking* anything, just playing a little golf. It wasn't our fault some people got all uptight over the littlest things.

The first hole teed off from my front yard, then doglegged slightly left to a tree on the boulevard about a block away. It was a par three; you had to play the bounce on the fairway (street) off the tee shot and chip over some bushes in front of the boulevard we called a green. Proper placement of the tee shot was key on this hole; if you hit too far to the right, your ball rolled into a sewer. Too far left, and you were in the neighbor's yard—which belonged less to the neighbor and more to the neighbor's two large dogs. (The dogs might eat your ball, which was a two-stroke penalty, or eat you, which wasn't any penalty but very painful.) The hole was a concrete block stuck in the ground as some kind of surveying marker. It was small; overshoot your approach, and you're back on the street with a difficult chip to recover—or, worse yet, in the sewer with no recovery at all.

The second hole was a straightaway par three to the next boulevard, about 250 yards away. You teed off from a spot adjacent to the first hole and shot over the street. Large elm trees loomed over the green; too much loft, and your tee shot would snag the branches and bounce back onto the street—or get stuck in a squirrel's nest, resulting in an unplayable lie. The only salvation on this hole was that if the ball bounced behind you, the shot didn't count. Also, if a natural hazard like a squirrel picked up your ball and moved it closer to the hole—

which was a tree stump left over from the ravages of Dutch elm disease—the advancement didn't cost a stroke.

As with the second hole, the tee box for the third hole was just adjacent to the green and was a bare spot strewn with woodchips. The third hole doglegged slightly left with about a 120-yard carry uphill over the street, to a boulevard in front of a brown ranch-style home surrounded by bushes. Your second shot was onto their front lawn; the hole was a tree in the middle of the yard. The tree—er, hole—was surrounded with landscaping bricks, thus making for a tricky putt. If you were short, the ball could ricochet under the bushes next to the house, rendering a three for par difficult.

The fourth hole was the highest handicap hole on the course, yet the par three wasn't too difficult for the experienced linkster. The tee was on the boulevard, beside the third green, and the green was a straight shot up the street, with sidewalks on either side to play the bounce for additional yardage. There were only two hazards on this hole: a couple of dogs in one of the houses on the fairway, and an irate old lady who called us hooligans and trespassers (and usually threatened to call the cops). I don't know if she ever did, but we decided a ball in her yard was an unplayable lie—you had to pick up, sprint across the street, drop, and shoot quickly, with the addition of one penalty stroke. Also, you had to rush your shot, and the approach to the green (which was the lawn in front of the junior high school) wasn't always accurate; the ball could easily land in the street, costing you even more strokes. To play the hole perfectly, you had to make the green in regulation two and then chip into the hole, which was a wooden plaque that read "Jefferson Junior High." (If you hit the plaque anywhere, it counted; even better, if you hit inside the *o* in Jefferson, you got to subtract a stroke.)

The fifth hole was an extremely difficult par three that doglegged to the right, starting with a blind shot off the lawn in front of the junior high school. You had to get it up in the air quickly to get a beneficial bounce off the back side of the school's sloping steel corrugated roof. A straight shot was also necessary, and the ball would land in the fairway on the other side. Hit the ball too far right, and you were in the parking lot. The lot was usually full of cars, which typically meant a one-stroke penalty for "vehicular denticide"—or a call of "game over, run like hell" for a cracked windshield. If you pulled it left, you were in the courtyard behind the building, possibly under a bench or in a flower bed. It was here that the experienced linkster would select a low-compression ball (for bounce) and generate enough loft so that the ball hit the roof just after the apex of the ball's ascension. This kept the ball from descending too fast and prompted a straight bounce over the courtyard and into the fairway for a clear shot into the green. Without the proper amount of loft, the ball either died and rolled down the roof into the courtyard or caromed into the parking lot. The key to this hole was the tee shot. Once you had made the fairway—if you made the fairway—the approach to the green was a seventy-or eighty-yard chip that left you one put away from the hole—a baby elm tree.

Hole number six was a beast. It was a long par five that doglegged left over water to a tight fairway with four two-story colonials on either side. The tee shot was from behind the junior-high baseball diamond to the backyard of the house across the street. It was important to keep the shot low to stay under the majestic old elm trees in front of the house; you couldn't go over them without landing in the common pond that bordered several backyards. The second shot was over the pond—with a fade left, if possible—to land in the middle of the fairway (also known as someone's backyard). It was important to remember that, after your tee shot, there were no sidewalks or streets to bounce off. Once, I saw a westerly gust take Bruno's second shot over the pond and bounce it off the bronze fascia above one colonial's picture window. However, that was a fluke; the only sure thing was the six to eight hundred dollars' damage that would have resulted from that ball hitting the window. The third shot was between two houses, toward the street. The hole was the orange warning light atop a construction sawhorse in the middle of the street, which warned motorists of ongoing repairs in the area. We decided it was sufficient to hit the sawhorse itself. The light was too small, for one thing; for another, we didn't want to risk shattering the warning signal and committing vandalism. After all, we were aspiring junior golfers, not accomplished juvenile delinquents.

You had to walk and then climb a little to reach the seventh tee. The golf architect who had designed the course—Bruno—had tried to add a little character by elevating the tee. The launching pad, or tee box, was on the roof of the kindergarten across the street. It was a flat, tar roof with a gravel top layer, and the hole—a tree on someone's front lawn—was about one hundred yards away. It was important to connect with the ball cleanly, or you might put a divot in the tar and spray little pebbles into your own face—not to mention dub the shot. The technique involved in this was extremely difficult, because you weren't allowed to dig one of those little wooden tees into the tar for fear of creating a leak in the roof. On one hand, we considered digging into the roof with a little pointed stick to be vandalism; the other hand, we figured a divot in the tar was an act of golf.

Immediately after teeing off, you jumped off the roof, club in hand, and sprinted to the next shot. (We figured that hitting golf balls off the kindergarten roof—not to mention trespassing—was a little conspicuous and might draw some unwanted attention. I don't know why we were so concerned with trespassing on that particular hole; every hole included trespassing somewhere.) Nevertheless, with a good tee shot, it was easy to chip onto the green (someone's front yard) and make the par three by bouncing the ball off one of those little lawn statues. This one was a little black man who stood about three feet tall and was dressed in a red coat; short, white knickers; and a black baseball hat. I think it was a jockey or stable boy or something like that. This choice of character struck me as strange, because there weren't any horses around, or a corral, or anything else that looked remotely equine.

Number eight wasn't designed to be especially difficult, but depending on the time of year, it could be a challenge. The tee was across the street, and no climbing was necessary to get to it. The drive was back over the street, about a hundred yards, to a boulevard, from which you'd chip onto the green. The challenge on this par three involved a ginkgo tree that in the fall dropped little yellow bulbs, which smelled like dog shit, all over the green. Not only did you have to chip over these little yellow stink bombs, but you had to endure what smelled like the men's restroom at the end of a Bears game. Concentrating long enough to make the putt without rushing your shot and blowing it—or puking in your back swing—was not easy.

The ninth hole was a pristine par three down the street and over the bushes at the corner. It finished with a slight dogleg left in front of the clubhouse (also known as my parents' house) on my front lawn. It was tough to play the street on this hole, because the road was sloped and usually covered with small pebbles we put there to trip skateboarders who frequented our fairway. The tee shot had make it over the street and land in front of the bushes for a clear shot to the green; hit it too short, and you'd bounce in the street and risk ricocheting onto the neighbor's front yard. Such a detour normally wouldn't be a problem, but these neighbors had a big Saint Bernard that took a dump at least seven times a day, and little brown bunkers were scattered throughout. The rules clearly stated that you had to play the ball where it lay, and dog crap wasn't considered a man-made hazard. Sometimes it was wiser to take the one-stroke penalty for a free drop than chip out of a pile of poop. Once the ball made it onto the green (my front lawn), it was easy to hit the base of the elm tree to finish the hole.

After all nine holes were played, it was customary for all golfers to meet in the basement, add up their scorecards, and partake of some libations.

Many great ideas, such as BOW and the tunnel, had been spawned in that very basement. Our latest product of delinquent creativity had been no exception. At that time, everywhere you went, golf was either being talked about or somehow advertised, with the Western Open scheduled in a nearby suburb for the Fourth of July weekend. There were signs promoting the event in shopkeepers' windows, and some of the more socially astute personages in town received invitations to corporate hospitality tents on the course for free booze and food while they watched the tournament.

We decided to hop on the PGA bandwagon and hold our own holiday tournament on the same weekend. Sure, we didn't have any tour pros at our tournament, but people wouldn't have to drive much of a distance or fight the crowds to watch us. They could relax in the confines of their own homes as we chipped and chopped through their front lawns, and some could laugh as their dogs chased us.

Our event was sure to be fun for everyone. Yet…it felt as if we needed a little something extra to make this a really special occasion. We didn't have any corporate hospitality tents, or a gallery, or even a real golf course, but we did have ourselves. After BOW and the tunnel, we were legends in our own minds; to us, our participation should be enough to make this a rather special event. After all, what really mattered was our celebrity presence and our contribution to the festive atmosphere of this gala event.

Therefore, in the ceremonial spirit, we decided to dress up for the event. We would wear fashionable golf attire: mismatched outfits of colorful shirts and slacks. (When it came to golf, our fashion icon was Rodney Dangerfield in *Caddyshack*.)

"If we're gonna make this thing a real golf tournament, we should get caddies," Bruno suggested. "What about our little sisters, Bubbles and Peaches?"

"What do we need caddies for?" I asked. "You only have to carry one club."

"Yeah, but who's gonna carry your beer?" Bruno inquired.

"They don't let the players have beer on the course at a golf tournament," Mickey stated.

"They will at this one," Bruno quickly replied.

"Well, if we're gonna have refreshments on the course, we might as well have caddies in bathing suits," suggested Mickey.

"There's no way my sister is wearing a bathing suit!" Bruno's tone was emphatic. "This is a golf tournament, not the Sugar Shack. The girls will wear long underwear, and the male caddies will wear those white hazardous-materials jumpsuits, like at the Masters."

"Sounds like a plan," Mickey said. "Spread the word: balls in the air Sunday at noon, and brats and beer will be served with the closing ceremony that evening. We'll make the entry fee five bucks and a six-pack. We'll use the money for the brats, and anything left over will go to the winner. The more players, the bigger the purse. So let's get to work." He delivered his speech in a take-charge tone.

I was working as the night watchman at a construction site that summer, but during the Western Open, my assignment changed to guarding the clubhouse where they were playing the Western, at Butler National Golf Course. I don't know what I was guarding it from.

Most of the pros were either gone or just leaving when I started work. But I did get to hold the door for Tom Watson as he left the clubhouse and went to the parking lot on Wednesday afternoon. Mickey, who'd dropped me off, saw Tom get in his car and drive out of the parking lot. Mickey decided to follow the celebrity to a nearby residence that was owned by friends of our parents. Now, technically, this was stalking, and Mickey was acting like a publicity-hungry paparazzi. However, Tom was more than gracious. He didn't call the cops; he even took a moment to casually chat with Mickey in the driveway before going in the house. Mickey told him about our tournament, the unique course layout, and our obvious infatuation with golf. Mickey then went for broke:

"It would be a true honor if a famous golf celebrity such as yourself would present the winning trophy. You could stop by after the Western, make the presentation, and have a succulent bratwurst and beer—on the house. It would mean so much to all those kids in wheelchairs who are attending our tournament, because they can't wheel those things on the grass at Butler." (There weren't really any kids in wheelchairs, but Mickey must've figured we could swipe some chairs from the local hospital and get guys to sit in them.)

Whether it was the result of profuse generosity, or just because he wanted to get rid of this goofy kid with a wild story, Tom agreed to stop by our house Sunday afternoon. This gave our tournament real significance. Not only did we have local celebrities (or, as some may have called us, local delinquents), but we also had golf legend Tom Watson involved, providing legitimacy to the whole event.

Players started arriving after church on Sunday at about noon. Twenty participants decked in obnoxiously uncoordinated golf attire showed up, entry fee and six-packs in hand, and the course was primed for tournament play—for instance, we had played Ding-Dong, Ditch that morning with the grumpy old lady on the second hole just to piss her off, so she'd add to the challenge by calling the cops if anyone played through her yard. Also, fresh gravel was sprinkled all over the street in front of the ninth hole, and we fed the Saint Bernard next door a few Baby Ruths to stimulate more little brown bunkers.

Increased holiday traffic in town presented a hazard on the second, third, and fourth holes, but we solved that problem with fore caddies and tennis rackets. The fore caddies stayed ahead of each foursome with tennis rackets in hand, and if a shot looked as if it were coming close to a car, the fore caddies would run in front of the car and swat the ball away. Yes, this did introduce the possibility of someone getting hit by a car. However, that was only a possibility, and we were willing to take the risk—especially since the risk didn't involve us personally.

After minutes of preparation and moments of competitive jitters, the tournament finally was set to begin.

"Hey, you guys, I brought a buddy from school. It's OK, right?" asked one of the players, Walter Worthless.

"Sure," I replied. "The more the merrier. What's the guy's name? I need to put him on this roster, just in case he makes the leader board."

"What the hell is a leader board?" Walter asked.

"You know, Walter—the big sign that lists all the leaders in the tournament," I replied as I pointed to a big chalkboard with several squares drawn in.

"Well, you better spell this guy's name right; he'll probably be up there," responded Walter. "He's a helluva athlete. He started on the Indiana basketball team that won the national title last year."

"What's the guy's name?" I asked again.

"Randy Whitman," replied Walter.

"I saw him play," Mickey replied. "He's good."

"Yeah, but can he golf?" retorted Bruno. "And if he *can* golf, can he do it on *this* course? This isn't some mamsy-pamsy gymnasium, you know. Out here, these guys are exposed to the elements—like dogs, cops, and gravel, not to mention brown bunkers that smell like shit. Yeah, he can play, but he ain't gonna get any special favors."

About thirty players prepared to tee-off as the July sun blazed hotter and hotter during the late morning hours. It was shaping up to be a perfect day for strolling the links, playing golf, and imbibing in necessary hydration. There were six groups of five. Each group had two fore caddies with tennis rackets and two or three individuals to carry beer. We used our powers of linkster intuition, as well as scores from the preliminary rounds, to handicap the better players and place them in the final group, like they do on TV. However, our goal wasn't maximum television exposure; we just wanted to string this thing out long enough for the Western Open to finish and Tom Watson to drive over to present the winning trophy.

As a matter of fact, after BOW and the tunnel, a few of the participants really didn't want their faces exposed to the general public, and we would much prefer that Tom do the honors. This tournament was for the players, the caddies, and the memories—memories of a sophisticated, socially acceptable game being played by some unsophisticated, marginally acceptable dirtbags amid the majestic mansions and finely manicured front lawns of our luxurious (but not ostentatious) neighborhood.

I was placed in the first group, along with the other hacks. After a couple of holes, the caliber of my group was crystal clear; and it was also crystal clear that we weren't going to win anything. We were playing the course, and the course was winning. For instance, on the third hole, Bruno's ball got stuck on the junior-high building's roof, and I shanked my drive into the parking lot and hit a car—then had to pick up and run to the next hole, suffering a triple bogey. What were we doing out there? It certainly wasn't golf—or even golf as we knew it. I don't know if it was out of frustration or inebriation or just plain ignorance, but we decided to add a little excitement to the round by chipping at each other just after the target hit his tee shot. The idea was that the player could fake when he was going to hit the ball, hit it, and then run off the tee, dodging little white projectiles. The balls would come from other members of the group, as well as caddies (and eventually spectators). Also, we all agreed that anyone who hit the target golfer got to take a stroke off their scores from the previous hole. However, because we weren't wearing helmets, hitting the target golfer in the head meant a two-stroke penalty. (The head was defined as anything above the shoulders or between the legs.)

On the seventh hole, our group escalated this latest manifestation of excitement (or dementia, depending on how you looked at it), and the contest to hit the target golfer as he jumped off the elevated tee became more important than the golf game itself. As a matter of fact, we couldn't even finish the ninth hole, because a bunch of spectators had gotten a hold of clubs and were chipping little brown bunkers across the street while we tried to putt. That was it—enough of this golf stuff.

We quit and went back to the sixth hole to watch the final group finish. The crude leader board, which was no more than a chalkboard appropriated from the local grade school, showed Mickey in the lead, with Randy Whitman, the star athlete from the Indiana basketball team, one stroke behind. They were just teeing off when we got there. As Mickey swung back, a bottle rocket whizzed above his head and immediately exploded with a neat little pop. *Where'd that come from?* I wondered—then I saw Bruno. He was crouched behind some bushes across the street, laughing and clutching a thin, metallic tube with faint wisps of smoke drifting from its tip. Mickey saw Bruno too.

"Missed me Bruno!" Mickey shouted. "Right down the middle! You'll have to do better than that, Smegma Breath!"

Bruno took that comment as a chal-  lenge, and on Mickey's next shot, *two* bottle rockets missed him by inches. Again, there was Bruno in the bushes with the smoldering pipe, laughing.

Mickey complained that he couldn't play golf like this, and that it gave Randy an unfair advantage. However, after careful consideration and consul- tation among the rest of the other play- ers, it was decided that bottle rockets were a legitimate part of the course and therefore a natural hazard. As a result, the barrage continued for the rest of the sixth, seventh, and eighth holes. However, Mickey seemed to be Bruno's only target. Randy Whitman was a guest; I guess Bruno was just trying to be a polite host.

It was on the ninth hole, with Randy Whitman holding on to a one-stroke lead, that Mickey retaliated. As Mickey teed off, two bottle rockets whizzed over his head and exploded—only this time, two more missiles came from the opposite direction and exploded just in front of the bushes Bruno knelt in. Behind a big oak tree across the street, Mickey's caddie held his own smoldering pipe. Mickey must've hired mercenaries.

Bruno didn't wait to reload. Instead, he grabbed a nine iron from one of the spectators and sprinted to the neighbor's yard, with all of its brown bunkers. From there, Bruno proceeded to chip and barrage Mickey's caddie with brown mortar fire. Suddenly, a huge explosion about ten feet behind Bruno inter- rupted the onslaught, and the M-80 sent canine fecal material flying in the air. At that moment, two bottle rockets whizzed by and exploded just in front of the big old elm tree that hid the culprits of the poop explosion that had ignited behind Bruno. A bottle-rocket battle ensued, and before any of us could get our bearings, a thin, blue haze had resulted from exploding gunpowder. The stench of dog poop also filled the air.

It was amid this ambiance of sophisticated golf-tournament prestige that Mickey claimed to beat Randy Whitman on the final hole and declared himself the winner, holding his club to the sky as a bottle rocket whizzed by.

Attention had obviously shifted to the bottle-rocket battle; golf became an afterthought. There were two teams—Bruno's and Mickey's—and I'm not really sure what the object of the new game was…or if there ever even *was* one. Maybe the goal was simply to light off as many aerial explosions as possible, tossing in a few M-80s and Black Cats for good measure. The blue haze of exploding gunpowder hovered in the air throughout the entire block.

The battle raged until a white sedan with a little white flag on the antenna that said "Western Open" pulled in the driveway. At that moment, the explosions stopped, and people gathered around the car to greet Tom Watson and welcome him to our battlefield/golf course. Tom may have been surprised by the smell of sulfur in the air or the thin, blue haze, but he didn't let on. However, he did ask where all the crippled kids Mickey had mentioned were. Bruno told him the kids had had to leave early to go to "wheelchair choir practice." The legendary golfer may have bought it, simply because it sounded too stupid to be a lie.

At any rate, Tom Watson stayed long enough to have a brat and present the winning trophy, which was a silver loving cup borrowed from my dad's office. We took pictures to verify that *the* Tom Watson really had been there, and then he got back in the little white sedan with its flag and drove away. Just as the car was pulling out of the driveway, a bottle rocket whizzed over my head and exploded. I looked up, and there was Bruno on the roof of my house, laughing.

Immediately, two more rockets flew from the opposite direction as Mikey retaliated. This barrage signaled that the war was back on, and the two teams resumed positions behind bushes and trees. Explosions once again filled the air. One neighborhood linkster (DeMan, another BOW alumni) climbed out on the roof of the clubhouse (my humble abode) and fired bottle rockets from that high ground. As the evening dusk fell, the troops were running out of bottle rockets, but Bruno and Mickey supplied each team with fresh munitions from a cache of Roman candles and Black Cats. Kamikaze candle kids would run at opponents, paper cylinder in hand, and shoot multicolored balls of fire at their fleeing adversaries. The only ways to thwart the kamikaze's attacks were to either barrage the assailant with Black Cats or hope he ran out of fireballs.

The battle raged well into dusk. Previously sophisticated golfers and their respective puffs of smoke were all over the ninth-hole fairway. Soon, amid the crackle of fireworks and popping Roman candles, the whine of police sirens could be heard, growing louder and louder. Moments after the sirens became audible, two patrol cars, cherries alight, arrived on the scene. (Well, actually, they arrived on the ninth-hole fairway.) The combatants scattered, diving into bushes, behind trees, and over fences to avoid detection. An officer got out of each car, flashlight in hand, and began searching for the perpetrators of this unauthorized display of gunpowder discharge.

It was dark by then, but I could clearly see (from a hole in the floorboards of the porch I was hiding under) a young female officer walking toward the bushes that Mickey, Maury, and DeMan had dived into. Suddenly, the effervescent crackle of a hundred exploding Black Cats erupted behind one of the patrol cars. The officer immediately turned and ran to pursue a rather bold Bruno, who fled the scene with quite a head start. At the same time, I saw Mickey, Maury, and DeMan scurry out of the bushes and run in different directions. Bruno's diversionary tactics had been heroic, but now he was the one hiding in the bushes, playing cat-and-mouse with the cops.

It was a clear night with a full moon, so I could see from my peephole a shadowy figure, who appeared to be Mickey, creeping toward the cop cars with something in his hands. Suddenly more firecrackers erupted behind the patrol car, and the officers chasing Bruno turned to chase the newest perpetrator. However, Mickey was already running and had slipped into the shadows of the house on the second hole.

As I silently sat beneath the porch, beams from the police flashlights panned the area, looking for Bruno and Mickey. The officers searched in vain for about an hour with no success.

Whether they were hiding from the cops or playing golf, Mickey and Bruno knew how to use course knowledge to their advantage. Then it occurred to me that our efforts to fashion nine holes out of our neighborhood to play a gentleman's game didn't necessarily make us gentlemen.

Perhaps we never became gentlemen like those Scottish aristocrats on the wall at my father's golf club, but we did grow up. Bruno, Rocky and Maury still inhabit the Chicago area and have evolved into moderately respectable members of their communities, complete with houses, families and mortgages. Mickey, Jimmy and DeMan live out of state and are also fairly well domesticated. As for me, the memories of sowing these wild oats still linger. I wrote these stories to entertain and enlighten readers, so they will better understand the oats their own kids may someday sow.

978-0-595-40615-9
0-595-40615-7

Printed in the United States
67571LVS00004B/553-558